FAITH IS POWER

formerly

Faith as a Constructive Force

SWAMI PARAMANANDA

Faith
As a Constructive Force

BY
SWAMI PARAMANANDA

Sri Ramakrishna Math
MYLAPORE MADRAS 600 004

Published by
The President
Sri Ramakrishna Math
Mylapore, Chennai-4

XIII-2M 3C-5-2005
ISBN 81-7120-234-9

Printed in India at
Sri Ramakrishna Math Printing Press
Mylapore, Chennai-4

CONTENTS

CONTENTS

I.

CONSTRUCTIVE FORCE OF FAITH

Thou seest, therefore, how faith cometh from above, from God; and has great power, but doubting is an earthly spirit and proceedeth from the evil one and has no strength.—*Shepherd of Hermes.*

Have faith in God. Therefore, I say unto you what things soever ye desire when ye pray believe that ye receive them and ye shall have them.—*Jesus the Christ.*

WHAT economic value faith exerts upon our life! Our modern life so bent on practical utility will have no share in visions and uncertain speculation. So must we not set aside the doctrine of faith as an ornament of a by-gone age? Yet in spite of all this barricade of material logic, the soul of man invariably turns its ear to the echo of the distant past,—"Verily I say unto you, if ye have faith as a grain of mustard seed, ye shall say unto this mountain, Remove hence to yonder place: and it shall remove; and nothing shall be impossible unto you." It leaves very little room for speculation. "Nothing shall be impossible unto you" is very definitely stated. Faith is a dynamic and a constructive force in our life. Through the exertion of this divine gift men have wrought miracles in every age and in every country. We may scoff at the very mention of faith and try to discard it from our highly civilized modern life, but in no way do we shake this eternal foundation of truth save to impoverish our individual life.

We imagine that faith cannot stand the test of reason. Faith and rationalism are not opposed to each other. In fact they supplement each other. The faculty of pure reasoning leads us to knowledge and knowledge gives us faith. If we put belief, reason, knowledge and faith together, we have the complete picture of mental phenomena. How our mind climbs from belief to reason, through reason to knowledge, and from knowledge to ultimate faith. Perhaps we can make it clearer by relating it to our every day experience. Sometimes we gain information through a trustworthy source and we say we believe it and are willing to make further investigation in the matter. But if the same information is given by an untrustworthy person and if it seems unreasonable, we drop it and no further inquiry is made. So first we believe because of the trustworthy source; then we exert our reasoning faculty; we strive and inquire, and as the result of this we gain true knowledge of the subject. Then we can stand up and say, I have absolute faith in this. If this is true in our material life, how much more true it must be in the spiritual realm. When we come upon the threshold of what science designates as unknowable phenomena, what better means can we

have than to place our trust in that part
of our being which does not come within
the evidence of our physical senses?

From the crudest concept of religion to
its purest and loftiest expression, tremendous emphasis has always been laid upon
faith. Throughout the ages we find num-
berless instances of miracles performed
through the power of faith. Are not miracles the working out of higher laws on the
spiritual plane? The man of consecration
who depends primarily on God, and knows
that he is sustained by the Will of God,
can perform that which may seem impossible or supernatural because he has uni-
ted himself with the basic power of the
universe. The skeptic, however, looks upon these happenings as brain hallucina-
tions, because he confuses faith with a
morbid idea of non-action and argues that
it is not for this age, that we cannot live
by faith alone. No teaching, however lofty

it may appear, however much it may appeal to the aesthetic or intellectual sense, can hold man's regard for long, unless it has a practical basis. Faith has found its fulfillment in the lives of the world's greatest men.

We are all creatures of faith. It is not that any of us fundamentally lack faith, but we all place our faith differently; and a great deal of our variance springs from this cause. Our devotion to higher ideals of life, or our lack of it, is directly due to where we place our trust. We are not attached to materiality through accident. It is because our inherent nature believes it to be of paramount importance. Our mind and heart will naturally follow their accustomed ways in spite of all our codes and creeds. We prove it especially in the hour of emergency. For instance, when a person is ill, he calls a physician because he has faith in the power of the physician to cure him. Whenever we are in need of human assistance, we call on those who can fulfill our requirements, because we have faith in them. Similarly there are souls who have unquestioning faith in God, and naturally in their hour of need they call on Him and receive their assistance from that divine Source. Faith in the Divine, however, can never be imitated. It must be natural, spontaneous and genuine.

We may ask, what is the philosophy of faith? It is most simple, but subtle. For this reason how often the worldly wise pass by its gate unaware of its benevolent power! That is why we find great men telling us again and again, unless we become like little children we cannot enter this holy kingdom of faith. But all our philosophic reasoning and genuine search will always lead us to the ultimate conclusion that the why and wherefore of our being is contained in the great Cause.

There is a great difference between faith and what people call belief. Belief is superficial and is easily shaken, but faith makes us strong and steadfast. We cannot have faith in God unless we know that He exists. We cannot have faith in the immortality of our soul unless we have an inner conviction of immortality. Faith is not an abstract indefinite sentiment to be put away on a shelf. At the outset it is necessary for us to exert our intellectual faculties to the utmost, but there are things we cannot grasp by reason only,— things which belong to the Infinite, and to these we can find our access more naturally through childlike simplicity and trust. A great Teacher once said to a disciple who was inclined to tear things apart intellectually: "My son, do you think you can measure the Infinite with a tape measure?"

Divinity is ever present in every heart,

but through our critical attitude and
doubting mind we often deprive ourselves
of Its beneficent Presence. Sri Ramakrishna used to say one finds God very
directly and simply through faith, but intellectual arguments only drive Him further and further away. How often Christ
said: "As ye believe, so will it be." A
man of faith constructs something beautiful even in the midst of chaos, while one
of doubting mind always destroys even
that which has been created for his happiness.

A doubting mind is a diseased mind.
We are able neither to receive a blessing
nor to retain it so long as our mind is full
of doubt and despair. Humanity finds its
best expression in those who place their
utmost trust in God and remain firm under all the varying circumstances of life.
In this age of materiality it is most inspiring to see a man who is willing to face

any difficulty, to lay down his life for the sake of his Ideal. The skeptical man of the world will not believe in the conquering power of such a life. He wishes to accomplish everything at once. He has neither the spiritual insight nor the patience to wait, and he who will not wait for the cosmic law to work out, always perishes.

The man who is full of faith in the Divine does not work for self-gratification. He has a larger point of view. He works for humanity. How could it be otherwise with one who has become part of God's plan? He has learned to offer himself in perfect faith and no matter in what circumstances he is placed, he never forgets that his life belongs only to that One. The man who stands on this rock of truth is unshakable. He is no longer connected with the small and the personal; he has connected himself with the cosmic force;

he has set his faith right and because of that he has become invincible. But placing our faith in God does not mean that we are going to eliminate all our troubles and tribulations. On the contrary, our test may be greater than that of others. We should be very glad to have hardships placed upon us so that we may prove our faith. People who lack faith are, as a rule, always faint-hearted. Whenever a difficulty comes or too much is demanded of them, they give way, because they have no trust in the infinite, inexhaustible reservoir of life.

Faith has a three-fold aspect. When we limit our concept of life to this little span of existence, we cannot help but doubt ourselves, doubt humanity and doubt God. These three go together. A man who has no faith in his own divine heritage cannot have faith in God; and a man who has no faith either in God or in him-

self certainly cannot have faith in humanity. Doubt throws the whole world into a
state of turmoil. It destroys the moral
fibre of humanity as well as the entire so-
cial fabric. Men grow suspicious of each
other and this suspicion is not limited to
a community or a country, it becomes a
world-wide disease resulting in war, intolerance and all kinds of hideous conditions. The starting place for all is the individual heart. Doubt is like a little germ
which gets lodged in the heart and infects
the whole being.

The degradation of the individual begins when he loses faith in the power of
God and no longer believes that he has any
access to Divinity. As soon as man al-
lows himself to believe that he is not of
God he cannot help but doubt himself.
As he doubts himself, he lowers his stand-
ard and becomes incapable of doing anything good or noble. The Shepherd of

Hermes tells us: "Turn unto the Lord with all thy heart and ask of him without doubting and Thou shalt know the mercy of the Lord; how that He will not forsake thee, but will fulfill the request of thy soul. For God is not as men mindful of the injuries He has received; but He forgets injuries and has compassion upon His creature. Wherefore purify thy heart from doubting and put on faith and trust in God; and thou shalt receive all that thou shalt ask. But if thou shouldst chance to ask somewhat and not immediately receive it, yet do not therefore doubt because thou hast not presently received the petition of thy soul."

We must have faith. Faith in what, you may ask. In the nearest thing we can find. Is our life so devoid of good that we have nothing in which we can place our trust? There is a divine spark in humanity and the man of faith finds it; not only does he find it but with his faith he inspires even the skeptical and the doubting. That is one of the greatest services the master-spirits render to the world. By their own faith they awaken the faith of humanity. They trust even the wicked who come in contact with them and they overwhelm them by their child-like, simple and unquestioning trust. Such souls exert a constructive influence not only upon individuals but upon a whole community. Faith regenerates. There is no limit to the power of the human soul. A man who thinks himself the most sinful of all sinners, fallen without hope, rises to his feet again when a wise and loving heart comes and rekindles in him the divine spark. No matter what he has done, no matter how deep has been his sin, he is redeemed.

You sometimes say, how can I believe in myself when I have failed so many

times? Do not doubt yourself. Do not
be conscious only of the material aspect
of your life; go deeper, to the Root, to the
Source. Are we not part of the cosmic
universe? No matter how small or insignificant we may seem at times, we are
always connected with the great whole.
That should be the starting point for our
thought and action. As we think, so we
become. If we begin by thinking we are
sinners, born in iniquity, we shall very
quickly become so. If we think that human beings cannot be trusted, because
they are evilly constituted, we do injustice
to humanity. But when people cheat us,
rob us, maltreat us, how can we place our
faith in them? There is a place in every
heart upon which we can absolutely depend. We must try to find that. No matter how degràded a person may be, there
is still within him the divine spark. If
we fail to call that out, we have failed in

our duty towards ourselves and towards our fellow-men. It may seem a difficult task. It is. It is no ordinary task. It is not for the person who is impatient for results and wants everything for himself. It is for those who have ideals and are ready to live and die for them.

We must learn to go deep down in our soul. As soon as we have found our centre of being, the whole aspect of our life changes. The person we doubted before, we now trust. The persons we shrank from, we now want to draw close to, for we find the same heart beating in their breasts as in our own. This discovery binds us to them with a bond of love. Do not lose your faith in humanity. The spark of Divinity is everywhere. It may not always be shining on the surface. But never doubt, because by doubting we hinder ourselves and we also hinder others. No matter how many times we may be deceived, we must make our faith more unshakable. Have faith in your spiritual being; believe in your divine heritage; remind yourself constantly that you are a child of God, that your life is not a matter of chance or accident, but that you have come directly from that one unchanging Source.

Faith is a marvellous gift. It gives us direct access to Divinity. Contrary forces may come and try to make us disbelieve, but we have felt and we have known. When we feel and know, we do not doubt. We should gather up all our effort in order to reach that point in our spiritual evolution. One direct glimpse of our Ideal will convince us. All the great personages in sacred history were men of tremendous faith in their spiritual power, in their divine heritage. Nothing could tempt them because what they had was infinitely finer than anything any one

could give them. They would not ex-
change their treasure for the richest material possession. It is said of Mohammed that his uncle tried to dissuade him
from his religious ardor, as it was making him unpopular among the people. He
offered him a large sum of money if he
would keep quiet about his faith. This
was Mohammed's answer: "If you gave
me the sun in one hand and the moon in
the other, I should not give it up." A
stream can never go backward. When
that stream of faith once begins to flow,
it washes us clean of all alien matter.

The more we know of the vastness, the
infinitude of God, the greater grows our
humility. There are certain principles
which go with the spiritual life: faith, humility and steadfast devotion. This devotion is not sentimentality; it is a definite
glowing feeling that arises spontaneously
from one's own inner depths. Without it

we lose much of the beauty of life. There is no happiness for the man of doubting mind either in this world or the next, because we carry to the next world only the things we have set our heart on here. If our heart is set on the small and ephemeral, if petty ideas overwhelm us, we carry those with us. Therefore we must begin to make a spiritual foundation right from the beginning.

When a man says "I can't", it is because he is depending too much on his physical strength and his mental calibre, and does not take into consideration that higher Power which sustains and directs him. Self-reliance and faith are not opposed. When we combine these two ideas we are invincible. God is ever seeking our co-operation and we must ever seek the aid and co-operation of God, no matter what task we undertake. When we place our trust in the Divine we can surmount all dangers and even death cannot thwart us.

One who knows definitely the majesty of his own soul and his alliance with Divinity never loses his courage or his faith. There are people who condemn a religion or philosophy without knowing anything about it, or even taking the trouble to investigate it. They think themselves very clever. On the contrary, they are destructive to themselves and to their fellow-beings. The Katha-Upanishad says of these: "Fools dwelling in ignorance, yet imagining themselves wise and learned, go round and round in crooked ways, like the blind leading the blind." Such people again and again fall under the sway of disease, death and affliction. A simple trustful nature carries us smoothly over the sea of life, but when we begin to dispute the why and wherefore of things we are overwhelmed. Once a man wanted to cross a river and a sage gave him an amulet and told him that it would carry him across the water safely. The man started with it and was surprised to see that he was able to walk over the water; but when he reached the middle of the river, curiosity entered his mind and he opened it to see what it was. He found only the name of the Lord Rama written on it and thought, "Is that all!" As soon as he lost his faith, he sank down.

Let us be silent and full of faith so that we can hear God's voice. This turbulent mind of ours plays havoc with us. It has power to create and also to destroy. It is one of the most potent instruments we have. We can so train it that it will be free from suspicion and doubt, full of trust in the Divine; or we can make it so unruly that it tears everything to pieces, even the most beautiful. We find people in the world who create an atmosphere of destruction behind them and before them and all about them. They not only have no peace in their own hearts, but they destroy the peace of others. For this reason Sri Krishna says with such dynamic force: "Cutting asunder with the sword of wisdom this doubt of Self, born of ignorance, lying in the heart, take refuge in Yoga of wisdom and arise!" It is good counsel for all of us. There are moments when we lose courage. The haze of doubt enshrouds our high vision and we feel downcast. But let us always carry in our heart the precious light of faith. At first it may seem very small, a little flickering candle light; but it will suffice, it will grow in volume, in power, if only we know how to nurture it. That is all we need to do.

Every one of us cannot become a master, but we can place ourselves with unflinching faith directly under the guiding hand of God; not with calculation, however, as to how much we are going to get out of it. Those who ask nothing for themselves are the richest. They have abundance to give in the way of love, life and strength, because they are not beggars. Do not let us be beggars. The Infinite is our heritage. As our faith in that increases, the less we shall feel oppressed by material circumstances. The heart of the mystic always knows this and cries: "Oh! faith, faith; oh! marvellous virtue, which illumines the spirit of man and leads him to the knowledge of his Creator. Oh! virtue altogether lovely, so little known, and still less practised, yet which, once known, is so glorious, so full of unspeakable blessing."

II.

FAITH AND SELF RELIANCE

Man consists of his faith. He is verily what his faith is.—*Bhagavad-Gita.*

The friend who will assist you is God; but to attain His friendship you must walk in His ways and place in Him the firmest reliance. The provisions must be faith and hope and the remembrance of your good works.—*Zoroaster.*

THE Bhagavad-Gita declares that the man of unflinching faith who has mastered his senses attains wisdom, and having attained wisdom, he enjoys supreme peace; but for the one who lacks in faith there is happiness neither in this world nor the next, because he destroys his own happiness by his doubting nature. Then in another chapter it says: "Let a man raise himself by his own Self". Thus in these two passages there seem to run two apparently opposing principles, one of faith and one of self-reliance; and the question inevitably arises in our minds, how can we harmonize these two? If we

have unwavering faith in God and leave
everything to Him as the only Doer, there
is nothing left for us to accomplish by
our own individual will. Where then is
the place for self-reliance? A man who
trusts in God cannot trust in himself.
Looking from the outside, these two
ideals seem to contradict each other; yet
there is not so much difference between
them as we imagine.

True self-reliance does not mean reliance on one's physical strength; it
means reliance on something mightier,
something which is less perishable. When
through discrimination we can realize our
identity with That which is Invisible and
Unchangeable, we are able to trust in
That and not become proud or self-satis-
fied. Often we think that if a man believes too much in his own power, he will
grow arrogant and lose his dependence on
God. That is true of an ordinary human

being who does not see beneath the surface of his nature; but one who has full use of his discriminative faculty and has learned to distinguish between the real and the unreal, knows where to place his trust. He bases his faith on the invisible and unchangeable essence of his being, which is not made of flesh, and thus he becomes truly self-reliant.

The Sanskrit term *Shraddha* has a more comprehensive meaning than the English word faith; it means a sense of trust in one's higher Self, in that which is more than body and which sustains the body. Until this deeper faith is awakened in a man, he will take the attitude of being the doer and will depend upon his own human powers, which will always fail him. True discrimination alone can show the way to true self-reliance, and also it alone gives us true faith. Do not imagine that any one can have true faith in God who has not faith in himself. The coward or weakling never has faith in God. He may pretend that he has, but he invariably falls when he meets with difficulties. It is only the spiritually strong man who can have real faith in God and faith in himself as part of God. Self-reliance does not mean arrogance; on the contrary, it may mean exceeding humility. Arrogance is the result of ignorance or the identification of the self with the body and with physical conditions; whereas the truly self-reliant man is one who has faith in his divine nature only, and therefore he can face even death without being moved, or frightened.

The dualist's point of view, that we should surrender absolutely to God and never exert our own will, is true; and so also is the monist right when he recognizes only one Principle, one Cosmic Power and that Power within man, declaring:

"Thou art That. Know thy Self, for thou art That which thou art seeking." These two conceptions are not antagonistic, they merely represent different stages of development. As our spiritual vision is unfolded, we come to perceive that every individual being is a part of the Cosmic Being. When we feel our separation from That and are conscious of nothing beyond our physical existence, our powers are limited and it would be wrong for us to take the monistic standpoint and say as Christ said: "I and my Father are one."

If we wish to invoke the Divine Being, we must take the dualist's point of view, looking upon ourselves as separate beings with limited powers, yet trying to invoke that which is Unlimited, Infinite, beyond all imperfection. At first we naturally rely more on ourselves than on God. As we go on praying and surrendering, however, and learn through success and failure, happiness and misery, that we cannot depend on our own strength, but that there is Something behind us by Whose will everything happens in this universe, we grow wise and decide to give up, saying "Not my will but Thine be done."

We cannot hope to do this at the very outset. As long as we feel that we ourselves have power to accomplish certain things, it would be a mistake for us to regard this power as false. What we should do is to relate this little power with the Cosmic Power. It is not wrong for a man to trust in himself, if he knows what is trustworthy in his nature; but if he trusts only in the false and unreal, then he is disappointed and defeats his own purpose. Self-reliance is not egotism. It means trusting in the spiritual, having more faith in that which is Imperishable and less in fleeting things. Such self-reliance, how-

ever, is only possible for the man who fol-
lows the path of righteousness. It is only
as we awaken the latent Divinity within
us and come to know our higher Self that
we gain true faith. Actually it does not
matter what method we adopt, whether of
faith or self-reliance; both mean a struggle
to relate ourselves with that One Being
whom we call God or Infinite Spirit or
Truth. It is One without a second; and
until we have established relationship with
that One, by cultivating moral strength,
we shall not find peace. But we cannot do
this until we are willing to live the life.
We must conquer all our lower propen-
sities, we must seek to discover that part
of our being which is infinite. Only so
shall we gain the courage and wisdom
necessary to carry us Godward.

So long as we believe in our heart of
hearts that our capacity is limited and
we grow anxious or unhappy, we are lack-

ing in faith. One who truly trusts in God
has no right to be anxious about anything.
He never loses his sense of complete surrender. This state of mind is not born
of any special condition of life, it is a
matter of individual unfoldment. A beg-
gar can have just as much arrogance and
egotism in identifying himself with his
poverty, as the rich man in identifying
himself with his riches; both are equally
far from the goal.

One who has spiritual vision does not
care where he may be placed; whether in
the midst of turmoil or in the quietness
of solitude, he maintains his inner balance.
We read in the Scriptures, he who is self-
possessed—that is, possessed by his higher
Self—and who by the sword of wisdom
has cut asunder doubt, born of the lower
self, has reached the highest. This is the
goal of all living beings. We are all con-
sciously or unconsciously marching to-

wards that goal; but unless we follow a practical method, we shall not attain it. No amount of theory or imagination can help us gain it. Every religion or philosophy offers us some method, based either on self-reliance or self-surrender, and it is for us to choose one or the other and practise it.

The idea of faith is often misunderstood by people, because they associate it with those who are ignorant, uneducated, and who have no power to investigate for themselves. But faith is not blind belief. It is never well founded until it is based on experience. Vedanta teaches that each individual must prove everything for himself before he can have faith. Realization is the basis of all true faith. Otherwise, if we merely believe without knowing, we are no better than the parrot who may be taught to repeat holy names, but who, as soon as it sees

a cat approaching, forgets everything
and only utters its natural cry. We may
have wonderful theoretical ideals; but
until we have put them into practice and
proved them by experience, we are power-
less to withstand the difficulties which
confront us every day.

A superficial acceptance of any religion
is not faith. Religion is never a question
of following a creed or attending a church.
Religion is something which every individual must work out for himself; and
we cannot call ourselves religious until
through our life we prove the reality of
God and the reality of our own soul.
Merely talking about lofty ideals does
not make us religious. Therefore again
and again we are reminded by the Vedic
Seers that we must live our religion, we
must practise. Until we have penetrated
to the depth of our being and perceived
our own possibilities, we cannot fathom

anything; there will always be many things which will remain obscure to us. Doubt of self rises because we do not know what we are. Instead of believing that we have a mighty, indestructible soul, we believe in death and are afraid to die. Our conception of immortality is based on words only.

We should try to get a glimpse of That which is beyond. This we are asked to do by all great Teachers. But how can we do it? Two ways are open to us all. If it appeals to you to trust in God and not depend on yourself, then do it. Even when you fail and everything is crumbling around you, hold fast to your faith in God; know that He is all-loving, all-protecting. If you can do this, you will find yourself protected and guided at every moment. If that Ideal does not appeal to you, then seek within yourself, find what is Real and do not be deluded by that which is perishable and limited. Some people are naturally over-active and egotistic and find it difficult to have faith; but if they can direct their activities inward and begin to investigate their own nature, they will in time through their spiritual seeking gain possession of That which is imperishable. Then they will realize what the monists declare: "I am He. There is no difference between me and that Infinite Spirit; for this body is not my whole being; I am Spirit, I am the Soul, I am one with God." Thus they will be able to shake off all imperfections and limitations.

Often people say: "I am all-Good, I am all-Truth;" but their actions betray them. They do not live out their words, and such theoretical statements weaken rather than strengthen their spiritual faith. One who recognizes the value of an Ideal should put it into practice, not misuse it.

What we need is to apply the ideals which are given to us in the different Bibles of the world and prove ourselves true to them. Difficulties are sure to arise, but they are not permanent; they come and go. Whenever we meet them, we must remember that they are born of finite conditions and are bound to disappear. We must maintain our balance and keep our faith unflinching.

There is but one goal; that is to transcend the limitations of our body and mind, and through our thoughts and deeds to strengthen our spiritual nature. Only as we are able to serve our Ideal will our limitations disappear. One who serves his Ideal faithfully will expand even though no one may recognize what he is doing or give him credit for it; and as he expands his Ideal also will expand. Until we can enrich our lives and make all our thoughts and actions worthy of the Divine Being, we cannot have true faith either in ourselves or in God. One who does not do right, who does not speak the truth, how can he have faith in anything? But when we learn to live worthily, faith in ourselves increases and faith in God increases in the same proportion. We believe then that we are children of God, children of immortality, that nothing can destroy us; and this idea at once takes away all our impatience and selfishness, all our jealousy, intolerance and narrowness. We do not feel any weakness, because we know that the infinite ocean of strength is flowing into us so long as we keep the channel open. We do not want to take from others, because we know that there are infinite possessions behind us.

As through discrimination and spiritual vision we realize our own divine heritage, we are able to take our stand as human

beings and as worthy children of God;
then only can we do our duty towards
our fellowmen. When we prove the
reality of our spiritual nature, not only
do we help and bless ourselves, but we
bless many. Think of the influence of a
spiritual character on others! It lasts
through the ages. The message which
Buddha gave five hundred years before
the Christian era still lives. A spiritual
Ideal always gives inspiration to others;
and whenever we begin to unfold our
spiritual nature, we bring benediction to
mankind. Therefore we must believe in
our power to unfold. We must become
more trusting in God and we must have
greater faith in ourselves. We must cease
to put our trust in things which are fleeting and perishable. At every step of our
life let us use discrimination, let all our
actions be guided not by impulse but by
wisdom, and let us seek that wisdom from
the Infinite Source.

III.

POWER OF FAITH

All that I have heard men tell concerning God, that I have read myself, or perceived of Him in my mind, cannot content me. Infinite is His perfection, how can He be portrayed, or how can man find words to picture Him? Faith alone can reveal Him or teach me what He is; by faith I learn more of God, and in a very little time, than I could do in the schools after many a long year.—*Brother Lawrence.*

Therefore, cutting asunder with the sword of wisdom this doubt of Self, born of ignorance, lying in the heart, take refuge in Yoga and arise!—*Bhagavad-Gita.*

FAITH is one of the greatest spiritual gifts. It is a living, glowing factor in our life. But we must not confound this faith with mere belief. Belief comes from reasoning and argument. We hear something which appeals to us, we analyze it, reflect on it, and at last decide that we may believe it. This belief, however, can be shifted. By a word some one can create a doubt in our mind and make us waver again. Real faith, on the contrary, rests on actual experience and when we possess that, nothing can shake us.

Before we reach this point, however, we may accept the word of those in whom we have trust. As when we are going to a strange country and desire information about it, we seek out some one who has been to that country and is thoroughly acquainted with it; so first of all we must turn to those who are acquainted with the spiritual realm and listen to what they have to tell us of it.

It is for this reason that we have Saviours and inspired Teachers. If we wholly rely on ourselves to discover Truth, we may choose a round-about way; but if we take their word, we may save ourselves much time and labor. We believe in them because a careful study of their life and words convinces us that they know, and we depend on their knowledge until we acquire knowledge for ourselves. At the outset of our spiritual study we are forced to accept certain facts which are based on the experience of others, but we must not stop until we have gained the same experience for ourselves. Faith based on the testimony of another is never ours, it is another's. Until we have made it ours through our own experience, we cannot depend on it. To be dependable, it must rest on proof and this proof must be of our own making.

Unless we have faith we cannot work well, because doubt scatters and dissipates our energy. A little doubt enters our mind and soon a great storm is raging inside, which leaves us dejected and exhausted. Doubt always tears down, it is wasteful and destructive; while faith is constructive. It is so easy to doubt; for as soon as we begin to doubt regarding one thing, that leads to doubt of everything. Before long the whole moral nature becomes diseased. When we doubt, we strike a death-blow at the very root of the tree of our life and naturally all the leaves and flowers fade away. "The ignorant, the faithless and one of doubting mind perishes. There is neither this world, nor the next, nor any happiness for the doubting self," the Bhagavad-Gita declares. One who is full of doubt invariably misses the goal of existence, because he fails to take advantage of the opportunities which come to him. Without faith we can accomplish very little in this life. When we begin to practise, we find that it is always more beneficial to have faith than to hold a doubting, critical attitude. We must, of course, use our discriminative faculty; but to tear down does not show superiority. Those who criticize do great harm. They may drop just one doubting thought into a mind and that may grow until the mind is ruined.

A wise Teacher has said that if we wish to advance, we must take the road of faith. If we doubt, we shall go down and down. The doubt which leads us to investigate is all right; but when by the light of our soul we gain some deeper revelation, then we must throw doubt away. There are people who seem to be naturally skeptical; but their skepticism is nothing but a habit which they have cultivated and it can be replaced by another more constructive habit. It is just as easy to trust as not to trust. At the present moment we have faith in ordinary things. We have firm faith in the existence of this external phenomenal world; and if some one comes and tells us that it is temporary and apparent, we refuse to listen to him. We cannot disbelieve its existence, because we have based our whole life on a belief in its reality.

It is only regarding the realm of spiritual consciousness that we allow ourselves to doubt, and some of us even take pride in our skeptical attitude. We say we cannot accept what cannot be proved by the senses; but if we reject everything not proved by our sense-perceptions, we would reject a large part of the world. We do not hesitate to question the existence of our soul, but we never doubt our bodily life; yet a man does not live because he has a body, but because he is a soul. We may have thousands of bodies, but we never have more than one soul. For the sake of that soul we must strive to gain faith in spiritual realities. We must cultivate a sense of consecration and learn to trust in God even in the darkest moments. If we can do this, we shall be able to stand up and bear the most overwhelming misfortune.

We must never lose faith in God, in ourself, or in humanity; for in this three-fold faith lies the secret of all strength and all higher attainment. Whatever we think we become; if we constantly think ourselves insignificant and worthless, we shall become that. Man must possess faith in himself, but not in an egotistical sense—not as a person with a certain name and form, born in such a family and with a certain position in his community. It is in his higher Self that he must have faith—in himself as a child of God, a direct heir to Divinity. He must base his faith on that soul power within, which nothing can daunt. Then when he has learned to have faith in his own soul, he will begin to have faith in God, for we cannot have trust in one without having trust in the other. Have faith in yourself, in your vocation and in the Divine. A man who has lost all faith

in himself is helpless; no one can help
him and he goes to his ruin. This may
seem confusing—we must have faith in
ourself and yet we must give up all
thought of self. What does it mean? It
means that we must forget the lower self
and place our faith in the higher Self. The
faith which we now have in our physical
being must be spiritualized.

One cannot have faith without optim-
ism. Faith and hope are inseparable.
Depression is a great obstacle in the
spiritual life and we must strive to conquer it. People who are morose will find
it very difficult to advance. Cheerfulness
is one of the essential spiritual qualities.
We must guard ourselves against dejection, self-denunciation, or even feeling
a little down-hearted. When these feelings come, it is good to have some
strengthening text to repeat. "Though
thou mayest fail hundreds of times, let

not defeat frighten thee, child," were the
words of a great man in India. If we
yield to depression, we are easily un-
nerved by difficulties and we create more
difficulties. Dejection invariably distorts
our vision. It magnifies our troubles. It
makes every obstacle look insurmount-
able. That is why in the Bhagavad-Gita
Sri Krishna tells Arjuna that any one
who wishes to save himself must never
allow depression to possess his mind. If
he does, he becomes his own greatest
enemy. Sometimes this depression is
physical, sometimes it is mental, and
sometimes it is spiritual. Doubt in regard to our Ideal, lack of trust in God,
are forms of spiritual depression and they
demoralize our life very quickly. The
more active we are on the spiritual plane,
however, the less susceptible we shall be
to these dark hours of doubt. Never be
disheartened and never give up. Keep

your heart so pure, humble and free from egotism that when the great blessings come, you will not lose them.

Faith is born of contact. How can we expect the finite mind to come in contact with the Infinite? As well expect to put a gallon in a pint vessel, you may say. Yes, but the finite mind can be unfolded gradually and led to see things from a broader standpoint. Then as its vision expands, its faith will grow. Actually all men have the elements of faith in them. Some have firm faith in their physical strength, others in their intellectual power; but the truly strong man is he who has faith in his spiritual nature. If we know that there is within us a living Spirit which is undying, unalterable, we learn to trust in that rather than in fleeting material things; and when our faith in the soul becomes greater, naturally we give less importance to passing physical conditions and are not so easily conquered by them.

This higher faith, however, can only come by living the life. We may say that we believe in God and in soul, but unless our life shares in that belief, it is useless. Only as we embody our belief in our daily life do we acquire a firm conviction about anything. We must strengthen our spiritual consciousness and feed this as we feed the physical body. We must not starve our Spirit. The spiritual life is absolutely essential to our existence; and to make our spiritual life potent, we must be wakeful and we must have sincere yearning for the Truth. Life is wonderfully balanced by God-consciousness. If we give attention only to the material side, we are easily overwhelmed by doubt and despair; but when we care for the God side too, then nothing can overwhelm us.

A life which is based on true faith is bound to bring great blessing and to manifest great spiritual power. We cannot expect to gain such unbroken, unwavering faith at once; but if we seek and pray and really yearn for it from the depth of our being, the way will open by which we shall inherit this rare spiritual gift. When it comes, it will lead us to that realm of Reality which never fails, which never deceives, which is more real than this world, and which is the very foundation of our being.

IV.

FAITH AND SUPERSTITION

The heart of love and faith spreads, as it were, a beneficent shade from the world of men to the world of gods.—*Buddha.*

Consider therefore this doubting how cruel and pernicious it is; and how it utterly roots out many from the faith, who were very faithful and firm. Put on a firm and powerful faith; for faith promises all things and perfects all things.—*Shepherd of Hermes.*

THE direct vision of Truth alone can give us the stamp of authority in the spiritual kingdom. Whenever we make statements concerning the invisible realm, doubt, suspicion, even opposition often arise in the minds of others; and only when we have had the actual perception of the things of that realm, can we stand with firmness and determination. The mere collecting of facts from books or other external sources is not enough to give us genuine faith; therefore, we cannot expect any one else to be convinced by our words until we ourselves have gained conviction through direct experience. Our words never carry any weight until our thoughts are pregnant with wisdom, and wisdom is the outcome of actual vision. When we know a thing definitely, even if the whole world rises in opposition, we cannot be shaken or made to believe otherwise.

Dogmas and doctrines, ceremonies and rituals are only to help us gain this realization of Truth, upon which our faith must rest. Every church has its rituals; but this ceremonial side is observed merely in order to lead us to higher understanding. So long as we follow these forms with the right spirit, we have true faith; when, however, we forget the real aim of these outer observances and go through them mechanically, then it becomes superstition. All great teachers have prescribed certain rules and regulations for worship in order to bring out

real devotion in our hearts and so make
us perfect. But when we lose sight of the
true meaning of these rules and merely
follow them out of habit or from tradition,
then we grow superstitious and reap no
spiritual benefit.

The true value of worship lies in the
mental attitude and not in the outward
action. The thought is the leading power. When we do anything with the right
thought, only then do we get the right result. Otherwise we gain nothing. Thus
in the temples they wave lights, place
flowers, burn incense; but all these things
have no value apart from the inner feeling which first prompted them. Unless
the love of the heart gives life and sub-
stance to these outer forms, they are dead
and fruitless. "God is a Spirit; and they
that worship Him must worship Him in
spirit and in truth." The worship of God
must be living, for God is a living God

and the devotee must worship Him with
a living spirit of faith and love. When
we offer a flower at the feet of the Ideal,
that flower is the symbol of the devotion
of our hearts; and when we do not have
that devotion, even if we buy all the flowers in the world and offer them, we profit
nothing. In the same way, the candles
symbolize the light of wisdom. If we
have a clear understanding of this and
light the candles on our altar with full
consciousness of the meaning of the act,
then we gain the light of wisdom and all
the clouds of doubt and ignorance are
dispelled.

So-called intellectual people often criticize those who observe these forms and
have faith in God, considering them irrational and unthinking. But which one is
really unthinking and irrational,—the
man who trusts in the Infinite and Unchangeable or he who clings to the

changeable and the finite? Every man
and woman with any experience what-
soever must know the fleeting and unsat-
isfying nature of all external objects; yet
how often people blindfold their reason
and continue to act along the line of habit and tradition, knowing it to be contrary to their higher understanding. What
can be more truly a superstition than
this? Taking the unreal for the real, the
untrue for the true, or calling things by
false names is always superstition wher-
ever it is to be found.

There are very few in this world who
can differentiate real from unreal and
fewer still who have the courage to follow the real. Again and again in life we
get a glimpse of Truth; but overpowered
by prejudices or past habits of thought,
we fail to retain it. Each experience gives
us a new lesson in right discrimination
and yet how persistently we refuse to

learn it. Every death, for instance, reminds us of the uncertainty of our life, and awakens a momentary desire for knowledge and immortality; yet how often we try to cover the coffin with flowers and forget death.

This denial of facts merely because they are beyond the reach of our sense perceptions cannot arise from anything except extreme ignorance and egotism. Ordinary minds can recognize only things which are within the field of their present mental vision. Those who perceive merely the outer covering of nature, believe that that is all there is; hence when they pass judgment on spiritual things, they are unable to go beyond the threshold of outer forms and therefore regard all worship of God as idolatry. They cannot conceive any idea of life or happiness apart from their physical body and external surroundings. This of course makes them too limited to comprehend the attitude of a lover of God, whose whole interest is directed towards the essence of being. For this reason the mind that is dead to spiritual things can only comprehend dead, material forms or the outer image, while the devotee of the finer mind can penetrate the outer form and perceive the inner spirit. Hence that which is a constant source of joy and inspiration to the one is a closed book for the other.

Among those who may have some religious understanding there arises another difficulty far greater. When we are born and brought up in a certain creed and have formed certain fixed ideas about religion, we are inclined to believe that there cannot be any other way to Truth beside our own; and we become extremely narrow and self-centred. We look upon all other forms of faith as superstitious and false and condemn their followers as heathen and unbelievers. Such feelings, which often lead to hideous fanaticism and denunciation, arise from our partial vision of Truth. No one creed or set of doctrines or dogmas can represent the whole of the Infinite and we become irrational and really superstitious when we try to measure the Infinite by the finite mind. All condemnation, therefore, is superstition; because it is the result of ignorance and short-sightedness. The man of genuine faith, who has perceived the Truth directly, knows that it is the same Ideal which underlies all the different creeds and sects, so he hates none and condemns none.

Faith is a great thing. It is absolutely necessary for spiritual growth. There are, however, varying conceptions of what faith is. Some define it as trust in God or in a supernatural power, others as be-

lief in some special Saviour or creed, still
others define it as trust in their own
higher Self; but however divergent these
various standards of faith may appear,
the purpose of all is to uplift mankind by
giving a mightier Ideal to live by than
can be found in the physical realm.

To have faith in the great Saviours and
Scriptures is a fundamental teaching of
every religion. But why should we have
faith in these Teachers and Scriptures?
Why can we not gain the goal for ourselves? Because we are too weak to discover the Truth by our personal effort.
Our strength is not great enough. The
constant thought of the physical body
and the habit of identifying ourselves
with it has made us weak. But these
God-men, by their exalted living, have
grown strong enough to see the Truth,
and when we have faith in them, we actually see the Truth through them and by

their help. Just as when we do not know the way to some place, we require the assistance of a guide to point out the road; similarly we have need of these spiritual guides to show us the way to God. Truth does not exist outside ourselves. It is within, and through the aid of these wise ones we can remove the veil that hides it. They come to help mankind. Their whole life is a voluntary sacrifice for the good of humanity and so we can trust their realization. Believing in them, we also believe in the Scriptures, because all Scriptures are nothing but the record of the realization of these Seers of Truth. Having seen it, they have passed it on in this form.

We think we cannot live in this world without depending on external things. Parents bring up their children with the idea that they must have a little learning, a little money, a little pleasure in order to be happy and do their duty in the world; but these are all superstitions. To believe that we need the help of the external material world, is a terrible superstition. Matter to help Spirit! We ourselves must remember, and we must teach our children that we are not the body, we are Spirit, pure, immortal Spirit. Following the course of physical life, becoming a slave to the body is a superstition. To shake off this superstition we must have intense faith in ourselves, in our higher Self, which is immortal, indestructible and eternal.

A great sage, Vyasa, was seated one day on the bank of the Jamuna when some gopis came on their way to visit Lord Krishna. There was no ferry and they were eager to cross, so they asked Vyasa if he could carry them across. "Yes, but I am very hungry," he replied. "First give me to eat." They laid their offerings before him and he ate them all. With anxiety they watched him and then asked again how they should cross. Then he stood by the river and said, "O Jamuna! As I have eaten nothing to-day, so do thou divide thy waters and let these pass over." The gopis listened in wonder, remembering all that he had eaten, but the waters were divided and they crossed over. Vyasa had faith in his immortal nature. He knew that his spirit was birthless and deathless; that it never ate or drank anything; that it was above all physical needs; and it was of this nature alone that he was conscious when he spoke.

There are men who believe in their spiritual nature as much as ordinary minds cling to their external, physical nature. To spiritual men, the higher realm is so much more real than this, that depending entirely on that and remain-

ing in constant communion with that
is their natural state. Therefore that
which seems unnatural and abnormal to
the ordinary man is the most natural
state with the Seer. We all have some
sort of faith—but it is the object of faith,
or that on which our faith is fixed, which
determines the measure of the power de-
rived from it. The one whose faith is in
matter will have a fleeting and finite
power, the man whose whole faith is in
spirit will have unlimited power over
both the visible and the invisible. For
this reason faith has been declared to be
omnipotent. "For verily I say unto you,
if ye have faith as a grain of mustard
seed, ye shall say unto this mountain,
Remove hence to yonder place, and it
shall remove; and nothing shall be impossible unto you." It was His supreme
faith in His Father in heaven which en-
abled Jesus of Nazareth to perform all

His miracles; and this same faith in Christ Himself made it possible for His disciples to work even greater miracles.

Have faith in your immortal nature. Know that you are Spirit. Those who think that they are limited and mortal, that they are born and that they die, are superstitious. Anything that is weakening, anything that is degenerating, anything that tells us that we are limited human beings is a terrible superstition. By all the means in our power we must overcome it. Let us tear aside this veil of superstition, recognize our true nature, and know that we are eternal, imperishable and immortal.

V.

TRUST IN THE DIVINE

We sleep in peace in the arms of God when we yield ourselves up to His providence, in a delightful consciousness of His tender mercies; no more restless uncertainties, no more anxious desires, no more impatience at the place we are in; for it is God who has put us there, and who holds us in His arms. Can we be unsafe where He has placed us?—*Fenelon.*

He who can resign himself to the will of the Lord with simple faith and guileless devotion, attains unto Him without delay. He who has faith has all and he who lacks faith lacks all.—*Sri Ramakrishna.*

WE must never lose our faith in the Divine. It is the root of our being. When that is weakened, our whole life suffers. If through our own action or through what others say we begin to falter in our faith and in our relationship with God, we see darkness in everything. It is the greatest misfortune that can befall us. If we do not have faith in God and in spiritual things, that means we have more faith in the world. Our faith is misplaced. We believe too much in the non-essential, and our higher vision is obstructed. When people say that they have no faith in anything, it is not true. If they do not adhere to the Divine, it is because they are clinging to things of the world and making those real.

Our balance in life increases or decreases according to our feeling for things of the Spirit. We can never have an unbroken sense of the reality of God unless we have overcome the sense of the reality of the material universe. It is not that we destroy anything; but as we live our life in the world, we fill it with a new spiritual consciousness. To have faith in God does not imply that we lose faith in the world or in humanity; we have merely a better understanding of the whole scheme of life. We are strong in faith and independent of the world if we see, not the seeming, but that which stands behind it all, sustaining it. Now this sense of God's reality we can create, strengthen or weaken. If we live carelessly, paying little heed or no heed to our spiritual unfoldment, it grows dull. It is not that we can ever lose the consciousness of God, but it may be buried under ignorance. A person may become selfish or wicked. The reaction upon his moral being is greater than any punishment a judge might inflict. It shatters his moral fibre, overpowers him; but as he has caused his own downfall, so must he regenerate himself.

No one can make us happy. Others may say comforting things to us, or try to create the material conditions which they imagine will bring us happiness; but always there will be something lacking within ourself and that inward lack nothing external can fill. Name, fame, prosperity—we may have all these in abundance; but they cannot fill one part of our life, and until that part is filled we shall strive in vain for balance. We cannot have a true sense of balance unless we have an increasing measure of spiritual consciousness. But it is very simple to acquire, if we turn Godward with uncalculating faith—recognizing the all-ness of God, learning to depend more and more on Him and making constant thought of Him our first and foremost task in our daily living.

At first we may have to imagine. But how readily our imagination works in material things which are advantageous to us! Take a man who is ambitious to make money. If some one comes and tells him a most improbable story of how to grow rich quickly, his mind begins to work at once. He becomes full of unrest, it absorbs his whole interest. It is the same when a God-consecrated knower of Truth comes to us and tells us of the wonderful blessing to be found in spiritual consciousness. Those who are ready, their imagination is awakened; their whole being is quickened by it; they begin to think; and as they think and reflect and try to realize it, naturally they come closer and closer to it.

I do not mean that a religious life is based altogether on imagination, but in the beginning imagination will help. It is better to imagine something high and holy and spiritual than to imagine ourselves to be weak, sinful and sorrowing. Our mind can work both ways; and we find our perfect balance when the worldly consciousness and the activities of our physical life do not overpower our spiritual duties. We owe a certain obligation to our spiritual being; and when we do not fulfill it, we weaken our spiritual fibre and it suffers. It cannot die because it is immortal, but it can suffer through

our carelessness; and when it suffers,
everything suffers within us. We may
think that by caring for our body we are
going to be strong and happy. Many
people feel that if only they can have
perfect health they will be happy. But a
man's happiness requires a great deal
more than any material thing. We all
find it out sooner or later. If we live our
life thoughtlessly, we defeat our purpose;
because our faith in God becomes shat-
tered and there is no greater loss.

The spiritual life does not demand
that we give up everything. We give up
nothing, but we fill everything with rich-
ness of feeling. The idealistic thoughts
given by the mystics and seers and by the
Scriptures are only real when we make
them real. Otherwise they remain closed
books to us. We may say: "These are
very wonderful, elevating thoughts, but
they are not practical." We never know

whether they are practical or not until they have entered into our being and become a part of it. Sometimes our heart is closed, the door is shut and nothing can penetrate. We may be fortunate enough to come in contact with the highest and holiest, but we must have the openness, the readiness; otherwise we remain unblessed. If we allow our heart to be dry and barren, then even the grace of God, should it fall upon us, will dry up as water on desert land. Mundane things have a drying effect upon our soul. Everything becomes parched and thirsty within us when we devote ourselves to them.

Our faith in Truth can be increased or decreased. It is like a scale. If we hold our thoughts on worldly, material things and refuse to think of that which is higher and subtler, then our faith in the Unseen will inevitably diminish. You may

ask: "But how can we place our faith on
that which we do not see?" By our inward consciousness we can feel and see
and know it; but by our physical consciousness we can never see, feel or know
about God. The materialistic mind can
never solve the problems of eternity. A
simple person, full of faith, full of devotion, full of openness of heart, may know
a great deal more about God than a phil-
osopher with a brilliant intellect. Sometimes it becomes a greater advantage that
we know less, because we do not have to
unlearn so much. How often we wish
that we did not remember certain things.
Instead of inspiring and elevating us,
they hold us back. But this does not
happen if all the actions we perform in
life are done in relation to Godhead, with
a sense of consecration and the feeling
that He is the guiding Spirit working
through us, abiding within and without
us.

When happiness comes, we must not be elated. Let us be specially guarded then, that we may not forget and be carried away by the temptations and distractions of material life; because as soon as we lose our balance, misfortune begins for us. We may have worldly good fortune, but it is indeed a cloudy dark day for the soul when we lose sight of God and have not a clear conception that we are of God, that our life is absolutely in God's hand. If we have faith in this, then nothing matters. Dire distress, sorrow, calamity, nothing can overwhelm us, because we have transcended all sorrow in our consciousness. This is a much truer security than any we may gain by intellectual calculation or by material means.

A simple, trustful attitude of faith and devotion will always bring a feeling of the nearness of Deity. When we begin to analyze and calculate, God seems to go away from us. Why is this? If He is so near as we are told; if He is our innermost being, the Soul of our soul, the Life of our life, how can He ever go far away? He does not. It is our attitude of mind which creates that impression. We hold Him aloof from us by our own attitude. Sri Ramakrishna used to say that a man realizes the Supreme through simple faith; but as soon as he begins to argue God seems to run away. It is because he is trying to realize Him by the wrong method. When we depend wholly upon our own inferior faculties, we are unable to fathom the fathomless and we are filled with doubts and despair. But when with utter humility, simplicity and surrender we seek Him, very soon we begin to feel His protection and guidance.

Let us look up to the Supreme Divine Spirit with child-like faith, simplicity and

openness of heart.   near us.
He is within us. He knows our thoughts,
our feelings, our needs; and He will grant
us what is needful for us. All things are
possible unto the Supreme. At times we
may feel depression and a sense of inabil-
ity, but unto Him nothing is impossible.
If we can fasten our hearts to Him with
steadfast devotion and faith, then through
His grace all our imperfections will be re-
moved. Let us pray that our life may become more and more worthy, that He may
surround us with His tender blessing and
ever lead us by His protecting hand.